National Learning Association Everything You Should Know About: ROME Faster Learning Facts

By: Anne Richards

WHY IS ROME IMPORTANT?

Rome was at one time the capital of the Roman Empire located in the center of Italy and is one of the oldest cities in the world. It has been called the Eternal City and also is one of the world's most stunning places to explore. There are many shrines, wonderful churches, fountains and palaces that stand as tokens of Rome's past glory. Gleaming new buildings are a mark of the modern-day Rome.

WHY IS ROME A POPULAR PLACE TO VISIT?

As the home base of the Pope's, Rome also developed the center of the Roman Catholic Church. Today, millions of visitors come from all parts of the world to enjoy the lovely sights of many churches, ruins and prehistoric Rome. There is also a lot to see and many people go on a guided tour so they are sure not to miss anything. Visitors also enjoy the colorful life of sunny Rome as they stroll from end to end of the city's fashion shops and open-air market places and gallop in horse-drawn carriages.

ARE THERE ANY PARKS OR GARDENS?

Romans relish the city's many community parks and gardens, including the Villas which were owned by wealthy locals at one time. The great Villa Borghese has many hills, pastures and wooded areas that give a natural countryside feel. It also has a large zoo and the beauty honors the Italy's War so it is covered with important statues. The Villa Sciarra has famous fountains and a lovely garden. There are also beautiful gardens on top of the Janiculum Hill which are especially popular with children.

ARE THERE ANY THEATERS IN ROME?

The National Academy of St. Cecilia can be found in one of Rome's important Symphony buildings. The world's oldest Academy of Music is located in Rome and locals enjoy visiting the opera many times throughout the year. The Opera House offers recitals from December to June and during July and August, operas are performed in an outdoor location. Rome has many theaters that offer plays, musicals, comedies, plus many more shows for many types of genres.

DOES ROME HAVE ANY MUSEUMS OR ART GALLERIES?

Several paintings and statues are shown in the Vatican Palace and contain artwork by well-known artists like Leonardo DaVinci, Michelangelo and Rafael. Some of Michelangelo's work is painted on the ceiling and front wall of the Vatican Sistine Chapel. The national museum of the Villa Giulia has many different artwork from Italy dating back to pre-Roman eras.

Greek and Roman sculptures and other objects from ancient times are shown in the National Roman Museum.

WHY IS THE CATHOLIC CHURCH POPULAR IN ROME?

The St. Peter's Basilica in Vatican City is Europe's major Christian church and is decorated in an older Renaissance style. The church became popular during the time when Roman Popes gave people hope and love from many decades of war. Many people began to go to church because they enjoyed the positive light that the Pope tried to give the people which made many people come together. Today, these churches are still very popular and many of the locals are Catholic.

ARE THERE ANY PALACES IN ROME?

One of the most popular palaces is the Venezia Palace, which was built during the mid-1400's. The palace nowadays houses an art museum that makes it popular for visitors. There's also the Madama Palace, formerly owned by the powerful Medici family. The beautiful structure of the building made it popular and was also the household of the Pope until 1890 and the kings of Italy from 1871 until 1946.

WHY ARE THE FOUNTAINS FAMOUS IN ROME?

Many beautiful ancient fountains found all about Rome date back to the initial century, which make them very famous works of art. The Trevi Fountain, which was complete in 1762, has very large statues and architectural artwork. The city takes pride in these fountains making sure they stay up-to-date in order to keep locals and visitors coming back. A legend utters that visitors who toss coins into this fountain will one day return to Rome.

WHAT ARE THE SCHOOLS LIKE IN ROME?

The Roman Catholic Church runs a number of schools in the Vatican City where students take classes to become priests. Roman kids are required to join school between the ages of 6 and 14, which takes them through junior high school. If students join a public school following junior high, they would go on to senior high school. Students wage small fees to join these high-level schools but religious groups run a number of schools around Rome which cost money to attend as well.

WHAT SPORTS ARE PLAYED IN ROME?

Soccer is the greatest sport in Rome, as it is throughout Italy. Large crowds watch club and international soccer matches held in the Olympic Stadium. Horse racing, which is also very popular is held throughout Rome. Other sports comprise of basketball, boxing and tennis and many places to ride your bike. Did you know that the Sports Palace was constructed in 1960 for the summer Olympic Games and lies on the southwestern borders of the city?

HOW DOES ROME MAKE MONEY?

Most Romans make their living through jobs with the government as well as restaurants and trade goods. Many families have owned restaurants and shops for many generations which are passed down to other family members. Areas where there are a lot of tourism help the city bring in money. Rome also has factories that make clothing, textiles, processed foods and other goods. Motion Picture Production is a big part of Rome's income because it is a popular place to film movies.

HOW DO PEOPLE TRAVEL AROUND THE CITY?

Railways and roads connect with cities as well as airlines that can take people all around the world. Rome's Railroad Station is one of the major stations that attaches the railroad system to other parts of the city. Buses, cars, taxis, and trolleys likewise serve the areas around Rome. Established in 1973, all vehicles are not allowed to travel around prehistoric areas of the city in order to stop traffic jams, sound and pollution.

HOW DOES ROME GET THEIR NEWS INFORMATION?

Rome has many daily newspapers including the Messenger, the Time and the Republic that are published and read by many of the locals. Other ways the locals receive their information and news is through Italy's radio and television stations. Whilst most of the television programs are filmed in other parts of Italy, the radio television called Italiana has its H.Q. in Rome.

WHAT COOL THINGS DID WOMEN DO IN ROME?

Did you know that many of the women enjoyed to color their hair many different colors but the most popular colors were red and blonde. The women used goat fat and beech wood ashes in order to color their hair. A large majority of women who could afford to do this were wealthy and powerful families. Women in farming families were also known to color their hair because many of them owned their own goats.

WHY DID EMPERORS POISON THEMSELVES?

Although many people did not know this, many emperors would take small amounts of poison each day because they believed it would give them eternal life and immunity. Many people believed that drinking from the vessel from the horn of a donkey would give them emperors an antidote to save them if they took too much poison.

WHAT MAKES THE COLOSSEUM IMPORTANT IN ROME?

This large Colosseum has been ruined over the centuries from many wars but it still stands today in Rome. The Romans watched gladiators battle and fight large animals such as lions. These battles were meant to show pride and strength of the men. Nowadays you can visit this gorgeous Colosseum and explore what is still left over. This historic landmark has been popular for many years and there are dozens of movies which have been filmed here.

WHAT ARE BATH HOUSES?

During the Roman Empire times there were public bath houses that looked like square-shaped swimming pools and were surrounded by gardens, pillars and libraries. The bath houses offered warm and cold baths, steam baths and massages. The kings and queens did not use the public bath houses but instead had their own private area to bathe and relax. The baths of Caracalla, which date from the initial 200 A.D time are still very beautiful today.

WHAT ARE CATACOMBS?

The catacombs were methods of underground passageways that the Romans used, it was built from 100 to 480 A.D. The catacombs had many paintings on the walls and ceilings and with Christian codes and symbols. The most well-known catacombs were constructed by the Kings and Queens as a temple in honor of all their gods. The Triple Arch of Constantine, constructed around 315 A.D. is also well conserved. It includes three linked arches side by side, splendidly decorated

WHAT IS SOMETHING MOST PEOPLE DO NOT KNOW ABOUT THE ROMANS?

As many people might think the Roman Empire spent many centuries fighting battles, many people don't know that most of the Empire was against war altogether. The Empire felt they only needed to fight in order to protect their land. In fact, most of the Roman Empire spent a lot of their days building beautiful works of art like buildings and sculptures as well as roads. They spent years trying to build heavy duty structures to withstand battles and today many buildings still remain.

WHAT RUINS ARE FOUND IN ROME?

The ruins of the Golden House can be found in Community park which was the Palace of Emperor Nero. The ruins, which lie mostly underground has well-preserved artifacts from many different wars. Stairs inside the echoing marble column lead to the top, where a statue of St. Paul stands. The Mausoleum of Augustus is the tomb of Augustus and his family. Augustus, the first Roman Emperor, built this near the Altar of Peace after founding the Roman peace, which continued for 200 years.

WHAT WERE THE EARLY DAYS OF ROME LIKE?

A myth has it that Rome was originated by twin brothers and became the highest power of the western world. In the mid 500s, Emperor Justinian of the Byzantine emperor wished Roman rule of the city as a Byzantine region, but the decline of Rome continued. Rome had distant belief in the Catholic church until the Pope was able to turn the city into a better place which brought many people hope as they began to attend the churches every day.

WHAT BELIEFS WERE THE ROMANS PASSIONATE ABOUT?

During the time when the Roman Empire was popular, many people believed in Greek gods and goddesses to protect them. When the Romans were out at sea, they would pray to the god of the ocean named Neptune in order to keep them safe on the water. Many other temples were built around Rome in order to honor and show their respect to the gods and goddesses.

WHAT HAPPENED TO ROME UNDER NAPOLEON?

In 1798, after Napoleon took over the Italian Peninsula, the French troops attacked Rome. Napoleon did not like the Pope so he sent him to jail. During the early 1800's, actions for love and freedom from other rulers cleaned the Italian Peninsula. In 1848, Rome became a place for democracy and French troops took over Rome in 1849, the Pope then became a powerful leader again.

WHAT WAS CLOTHING LIKE IN ROME?

The Romans wore modest clothes made of wool or linen. The main outfit was called a tunic, which hung to the knees or below. During events, male citizens wore a toga, which is similar to a white sheet wrapped around the body. The togas worn by high-ranking people had a purple frame and it was against the law for non-citizens to wear togas in Rome.

THE POPULATION OF ROME AND ITS EARLY DEVELOPMENT

Rome has a large population of around 2.8 million people who live in the city which is located in the central part of the state. Rome's main goods are copper wire and many copper goods. Did you know that the city was first named Lynchville but it was renamed to Rome in 1819. Today, the Erie Canal Village stands on the site of the village and is a rebuilding of the area in the 1800's. Rome was united in 1870, it had a mayor-council form of government from that point on.

WHAT DOES THE LAND LOOK LIKE IN ROME?

The city of Rome was built on 7 wooded hills next to the Tiber River in Italy. The hills were steep and helped keep enemies away. The valleys had lush soil, as well as minerals for building. These areas of Rome were often harmed by damaging floods from the Tiber River. But the Tiber also provided a suitable route to the sea, which was about 15 miles to the West. The Harbor at Ostia located at the mouth of the Tiber river is a popular area for trading goods with other communities.

THE EARLY PEOPLE WHO LIVED IN ROME

Many people who first lived in Rome were from different backgrounds and lived on the Italian Peninsula, each with its own language and beliefs. The Romans were Latins and other main background groups included the Etruscans, Sabines and Samnites. The Roman Empire, at its peak, had over fifty million people with Latin and Greek being the main language of the Empire. The upper class spoke those two languages but all the others still used their native languages.

WHAT WAS THE FIRST ROMAN LAW?

The Roman Empire first started becoming popular during 27 AD. Emperors controlled the army and focused on making laws. The Romans printed their first known law in 451 BC, which was the law of the Twelve Tables. During this time the higher class made the laws in secret so many lower class people didn't know what the laws were. The Twelve Tables of Laws were laws that the higher class and lower class came up with together and set out on a stone for everyone to see. As Rome grew, its law system grew too and many more laws were set in place. Rome started the first specialists whose job were to understand the law on behalf of the people, which today are now called lawyers.

WHAT WERE THE PEOPLE LIKE IN ROME?

The Romans consisted of shepherds and farmers. In early Rome, landowners had crops in the spring and harvested them in the fall. The Roman calendar contained regular farming festivals. The game and amusement at the festivals offered a halt from the hardship and working the land. If you were not a farmer then you would be living in the modest houses which were constructed of sun-dried bricks. Wealthy families however, lived in nice villas, which were bigger and nicer than houses in the city.

WHAT IS THE FOOD LIKE IN ROME?

Most Romans consumed simple meals. Breakfast was typically a small meal of bread and cheese. Lunch and dinner consisted mainly of porridge bread, olives, fruits or cheese. Garum which is a pulp made of fish chunks and olive oil is popular as well. Wealthy Romans sometimes served dinners with many courses and the first course might comprise of eggs, vegetables, and shellfish. The core courses contained meat, fish, or chicken. For dessert, the guess would often eat honey sweet cakes or fruit.

Thank you! Thank you! Thank you!

It means a lot to us that you chose our book to spend your time learning with - we hope you enjoyed it!

All pictures and words were put together, with love, by experts from around the globe. Experts who love what they do and want to improve and educate the world, one book at a time!

We would really appreciate it if you could PLEASE take a second to let us know how we're doing by leaving a review on Amazon.

To leave feedback, Simply visit:

US Customers: https://amazon.com/feedback
UK Customers: https://amazon.co.uk/feedback

For all other customers, you can visit the "Your Orders" link from your Amazon menu and choose "Leave Seller Feedback".

Any comments you may have - what you enjoyed, any suggestions you might have and what you would like to read about in future books.

Any comments will help us understand better what you and your children most enjoy - this allows us to tailor future books and provide exactly what is most helpful and useful in the future.

National Learning Association

Made in the USA
Columbia, SC
22 November 2024